Who Can Go t

Can a cat go to school?
Can a cat do math?

No, a cat can't go to school.
A cat can't do math.

Can a dog go to school?
Can a dog write?

No, a dog can't go to school.
A dog can't write.

Can a monkey go to school?
Can a monkey read?

No, a monkey can't go to school.
A monkey can't read.

Can children go to school?
Can children do math, write, and read?
Yes, they can!